guide to

Santiago

80 PAGES. 75 PHOTOGRAPHS ▶

 8 MAPS, ITINERARIES AND TOURS

☐ Editorial Escudo de Oro, S.A.

guide to Santiago

3rd Edition

I.S.B.N. 84-378-1826-5

Dep. Legal B. 29012-2001

Editorial Escudo de Oro, S.A.

THE VISIT TO SANTIAGO DE COMPOSTELA

Santiago, the «City of the Apostle», which is, along with Rome and Jerusalem, Santiago, one of the three most important centres of Christianity, surprises and moves the visitor due to its monumental wealth. Its stones, carved out by the joint action of man and nature over the centuries, becomes art to move us with the spirituality with which it is imbued for, let us remember, Santiago de Compostela is a city built around the tomb of the Apostle Saint James. The beauty of its rich and splendid artistic heritage is enhanced even further, if that is possible, by that constant of the Galician scenery, the rain.

This guide aims to become the perfect travelling companion, helping visitors to get the most out of their visit to Santiago. To facilitate this, we have organised the most important sights into four practical routes. According to time available, visitors can link up one route with another, as the distances between the different points of interest in the historic city centre –almost entirely a pedestrian area– are not excessively great. A plan of the city, with these itineraries marked out on it, on pages 8 and 9, will help with orientation, and the guide is completed by sections on the history, gastronomy, festivities and crafts of Santiago de Compostela, as well as information on four excursions outside the city.

Statue of Saint James, in the Capilla Mayor of the Cathedral. ▷

Image of Compostela according to an old engraving.

HISTORICAL INTRODUCTION

The city stands on a hill with a height of 400 metres, and is 30 kilometres from the sea. It enjoys mild temperatures both in winter and in summer, but the main climatic constant is the rain, which acquires here, as is unanimously agreed, the «status of art», making typical the image of its streets populated by pedestrians protected by umbrellas. Situated in La Coruña province, Santiago is the capital of the Autonomous Community of Galicia, seat of the Galician parliament and of the Apostolic Archdiocese, as well as being considered the cultural capital of the community. It is a city of just over 90,000 inhabitants, though its position as administrative and cultural, as well as the goal of many pilgrims, means that the population is greatly increased every day. But Santiago de Compostela is, above all, a monumental city. In 1985 it was declared Heritage of Humanity, and the Saint James' Way receives the distinction of «First European Cultural Route».

The origins of the city go back to the year 813, when the providential discovery of the tomb of Saint James was made.

According to legend, the hermit Paio saw strange lights in the form of stars over the hill of Libredón (Campus Stellae –«field of stars»– from which is derived the name Compostela) an old Roman fortress. This unusual sighting was reported to Bishop Theudemirus of Iria Flavia, who discovered on the site a funeral monument containing the bodies of the Apostle and two of his disciples. It seems that in the year 44 AD, after preaching in Spain, James was martyred and his head cut off in Palestine by the Jews. His followers decided to place his mortal remains on a ship and head for Galicia. On landing, a

Main front, known as the Front of El Obradoiro, of the Cathedral of Santiago.

Aerial view of Compostela.

cart drawn by bulls carried the lifeless body of Saint James to the site on which his city now stands.

News of the discovery reached the ears of King Alphonse II, king of Asturias and Galicia, who ordered the construction of a simple church on the site, extended some years later under the reign of Alphonse III and consecrated in 893. It was during this period that the first pilgrimages began to be made, and Benedictine monks and settlers also began to establish themselves around the church.

One century later, in 997, the city and the sanctuary were destroyed by the troops of Almanzor, though Bishop Pedro de Mezonzo managed to save the relics of the Apostle. Rebuilt and walled shortly after, Compostela flourished once more under Bishop Xelmírez, a key figure in the history of the city, who helped complete the building of the Cathedral, embellishing it with new treasures, as well as being considered the artifice of the economic development of the region and achieving its conversion to an archbishopric by Pope Callistus II.

The city enjoyed another period of splendour during the 16th century, when Archbishop Fonseca founded the University of Santiago, an intellectual impulse which was matched by an architectural flourishing as between the 17th and 18th centuries many façades of buildings in the city were remodelled in accordance with the aesthetic criteria of the baroque style.

In 1879 the relics of the Apostle, kept from the public gaze since 1589, began once more to be displayed, coinciding with an important revival of Galician culture and heralding a resurgence of pilgrimages. The city walls were demolished in the 19th to permit the expansion of the city, whilst the 20th century saw the city's designation as capital of Galicia and the celebration of Xacobeo-93. These events acted as engines of change in this city, one which is both open to the future and respectful of its historic past. Recent years have, moreover, seen development providing the urban periphery with complete service and leisure infrastructure.

Rúa do Vilar. The streets of the historic centre of Compostela still conserve a strongly medieval air.

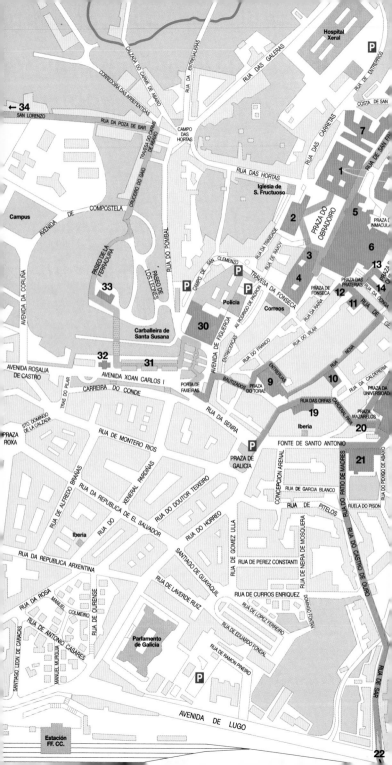

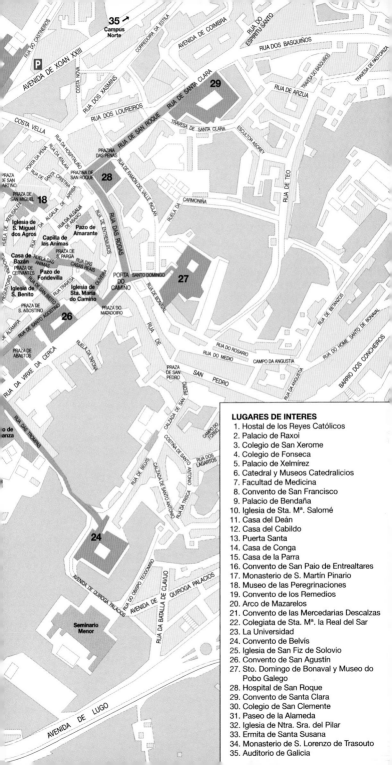

LUGARES DE INTERES

1. Hostal de los Reyes Católicos
2. Palacio de Raxoi
3. Colegio de San Xerome
4. Colegio de Fonseca
5. Palacio de Xelmírez
6. Catedral y Museos Catedralicios
7. Facultad de Medicina
8. Convento de San Francisco
9. Palacio de Bendaña
10. Iglesia de Sta. Mª. Salomé
11. Casa del Deán
12. Casa del Cabildo
13. Puerta Santa
14. Casa de Conga
15. Casa de la Parra
16. Convento de San Paio de Entrealtares
17. Monasterio de S. Martín Pinario
18. Museo de las Peregrinaciones
19. Convento de los Remedios
20. Arco de Mazarelos
21. Convento de las Mercedarias Descalzas
22. Colegiata de Sta. Mª. la Real del Sar
23. La Universidad
24. Convento de Belvís
25. Iglesia de San Fiz de Solovio
26. Convento de San Agustín
27. Sto. Domingo de Bonaval y Museo do Pobo Galego
28. Hospital de San Roque
29. Convento de Santa Clara
30. Colegio de San Clemente
31. Paseo de la Alameda
32. Iglesia de Ntra. Sra. del Pilar
33. Ermita de Santa Susana
34. Monasterio de S. Lorenzo de Trasouto
35. Auditorio de Galicia

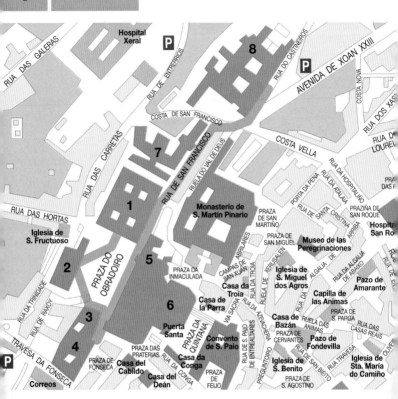

I. THE PLAZA DEL OBRADOIRO AND THE CATHEDRAL

1. Hostal de los Reyes Católicos
2. Raxoi Palace
3. College of San Xerome
4. College of Fonseca
5. Xelmírez Palace
6. Cathedral and Cathedral Museums
7. Faculty of Medicine
8. Convent of San Francisco

Thanks to the monumental buildings surrounding it, the Plaza del Obradoiro is one of the most beautiful urban sites in the world. Its name recalls the *obradoiros* (stonemasons) who lived here whilst they worked on the construction of the Cathedral. Now, a visit to the square provides the opportunity of admiring one of the most striking characteristics of Santiago de Compostela: stone made art. Rectangular in shape, the four constructions forming the square correspond to four architectural styles joined in perfect harmony and solemnity: the baroque, the Renaissance, the Gothic and the neoclassical. On the north side of the square stands the **Hostal de los Reyes Católicos (1),** also known as the Hospital Real, or Royal Hospital, as it was ordered built by the Catholic Monarchs to provide accommodation for pilgrims. It was built between 1501 and 1511, according to plans drawn up by Enrique Egas, and was reformed during the baroque period. It is now one of the most luxurious paradores, state-run hotels, in Spain.

Its broad main front features, besides the impressive main door, a stone chain linked by pillars that stand before it –in turn a symbol that royalty stayed in these apartments– the great balcony with four doors –the first on the left Renaissance in style, the other three baroque– and the large cornice with stone chain and disturbing carved gargoyles. The Plateresque portal is formed by a semicircular arch with a single archivolt

Hostal de los Reyes Católicos.

The Raxoi Palace.

and is flanked by the coats of arms of Castile. The medallions feature images of the Catholic Monarchs, Ferdinand and Isabel, whilst the spaces between the double pilasters contain statues of Adam and Eve. The little window above the frieze corresponds to what were formerly the royal apartments. Inside are four patios, two Plateresque and two baroque in style.

Opposite the Cathedral is the **Raxoi Palace (2),** built by Archbishop Bartolomé de Raxoi in the mid-19th century. Neoclassical in style, it was designed by the French architect Charles Lemaur, who took his inspiration from the design of the Paris Academy. It was originally intended as the residence of the Cathedral choirboys and seat of the confessors' seminar. After various uses, it now houses various departments of the autonomous government of Galicia and Santiago de Compostela City Council.

The most striking feature of this palace is the main front, 90 metres in length, whose central section has a lovely portico resting on majestic Ionic columns. The pediment, crowned by an equestrian statue of the saint, is adorned by a white marble representation of the Battle of Clavijo by José Gambino and José Ferreiro.

In the south side of the square stands the **College of San Xerome (3),** the simplest of all the buildings in Plaza del Obradoiro. Built in the 15th century by Archbishop Fonseca as a school for poor students, it is now the seat of the University Rectory. The front of the building was brought from a former pilgrim's hospital in the nearby Plaza de la Inmaculada, a fact which explains its decoration with the statues of saints traditionally linked to the health. Dating back to the 15th century, its Romanesque design is a clear example of the survival of this style even in the heart of the Gothic period. Inside is a peaceful, simple cloister, the work of Peña de Toro.

Adjoining the College of San Xerome if we take Rúa del

Portal of the College of San Xerome.

Plaza de Fonseca with the College of the same name.

Franco, and opposite the peaceful little Plazuela de Fonseca with its well-tended gardens, is the main entrance to the **College of Fonseca (4),** also known as that of Santiago Alfeo. On this site stood the bishop's place of birth, which he donated so that a school could be built here. Fonseca was also the moving force behind many other buildings in the city. Such was his contribution to the city's heritage that, in sign of gratitude, for many years a *sereno* (nightwatchman) called for prayers for the good bishop's soul.

The College of Fonseca was designed by Juan de Alava and Alonso de Covarrubias, in the 16th century. The Plateresque doorway is presided over by statues of the Virgin of the Pleasures and of Santiago Alfeo. In the tympanum are represented dragons defending Wisdom. The interior is organised around cloisters inspired by those of Salamanca, with cresting and fearful gargoyles. Also outstanding is the Aula de Grados, or Degree Room, with a spectacular coffered wooden ceiling following the precepts of Spanish Mudéjar art.

The College of Fonseca is considered the origin of the University of Compostela. It has, over the years, housed a variety of academic institutions, including the Galician Studies Seminar, which it now houses once more. In 1982 it became the first seat of the Autonomous Parliament of Galicia, and it is also used for exhibitions and as a library.

Back in the Plaza del Obradoiro and before visiting the Cathedral, we come to the **Xelmírez Palace (5),** built between the 12th and 13th centuries by Archbishop Xelmírez, though it has since been altered on various occasions. This palace is considered to be one of the finest works of civil Romanesque architecture on the Peninsula. Behind its austere façade are majestic rooms: a great hall, the Salón de Armas, and, on the upper floor the banquet hall, whose florid ribbed vaults rest on corbels decorated with scenes from history.

Banquet hall in the Palace of Xelmírez.

PLANO CATEDRAL DE
SANTIAGO DE COMPOSTELA

Capilla
de
Corticela

Capilla de
San Juan
Apó...

Capilla de
San Andrés

Capilla del
Espíritu Santo

Ca...
San

Capilla de
la Concepci...

Palacio Arzobispal

Capilla
de San Antonio

Puerta de la
Azabachería

PLAZA DE
LA INMACULADA

Capilla de Ntra.
Sra. de Lourdes
o Santa Catalina

Capilla
de la
Comunión

Capilla
del Cristo
de Burgos

Palacio de Xelmírez

P

Puerta
Santa

PLAZA DE
LA QUINTANA

Capilla
del
...ador

Capilla de la
Azucena o de
Doña Mencía

Pórtico
Real de la
Quintana

Capilla de
Mondragón

...illa
...yor

Capilla
del Pilar

Torre
del
Reloj

PLAZA DE
LAS PLATERIAS

Pórtico de
las Platerías

...oro

Archivo

Antesacristía

Ingreso al Claustro

Archivo

Sacristía

Capilla de
San Fernando

Claustro

Pasaje

Capilla
de las
Reliquias

la Gloria

Biblioteca

Sala
Capitular

...adoiro

Entrada a
los Museos

...la a la
...al Vieja

OBRADOIRO

Cathedral, front of El Obradoiro.

The **Cathedral of Santiago de Compostela (6)** is considered the most extraordinary monument constructed in Spain during the Middle Ages, and its most characteristic Romanesque monument. Construction began in the year 1075 and took just over one century to complete. The master craftsmen who helped build this great basilica included Bernardo the Elder, Roberto, Esteban, Bernardo the Younger and, later, Mateo. The cathedral's groundplan takes the form of a Latin cross with nave and two aisles prolonged in the crossing, ambulatory with apse chapels and triforium. The Cathedral occupies a total area of some 23,000 square metres.

The Cathedral **front,** known as the Façade of El Obradoiro, was built between 1738 and 1750 by the architect Casas y Novoa. It features constructional and decorative elements present in other churches the length of Saint James' Way. It consists of a triptych over a staircase with two ramps, flanked by two towers, originally Romanesque but converted to baroque in 1675. The right-hand tower is known as that of Las Campanas («The Bells»), the one on the left-hand side that of *La Carraca*, named after the rattle which is played during Holy Week. The front is presided over a statue of Saint James surrounded by various ornamental elements used forming a spectacular composition of lights and shades.

Under the steps is the entrance to the **Crypt of the Portal of La Gloria,** or Old Crypt. The design of the «Gloria Doorway» harmonises the crypt, portal and triforium, symbolising the Earth, Christ (the Redeemer in the Portal of the Gloria) and, above, the celestial vaults.

The crypt was built for the veneration and worship of Santiago Alfeo, a statue of whom presides over the entrance. Commenced earlier, the crypt was completed by the *maestro* Mateo. It is covered with groined vaults, whilst its groundplan reproduces that of the head of the Romanesque basilica. It is visited as part of the tour of the Cathedral Museums, and in it are exhibited various carvings by Mateo, and a series of panels explaining the process of the construction of the Portal of La Gloria and its symbolic significance.

Crypt of the Porch of La Gloria.

Porch of La Gloria.

Entering through the Obradoiro front, we come to what is rightly considered the most precious jewel of Romanesque art: the **Pórtico de la Gloria,** a magnificent sculptural work by the maestro Mateo. It consists of three archways corresponding to the nave and aisles of the Cathedral, interlaced by the figures of angels indicating to the souls the path to Glory. The arch on the left represents an allegory of the Old Testament, that in the centre, the Glory. The tympanum is presided over by the resuscitated Christ showing His wounds. The central

Details of the Porch of La Gloria, masterpiece of Compostela Romanesque art.

PORTICO DE LA GLORIA

1. Archivolt with eleven crowned figures
2. Christ in Limbo, between Adam and Eve and other Hebrew figures
3. Two minor prophets
4. Two minor prophets
5. The angels lead the faithful Hebrew people, in the form of children, towards Glory
6. The Just
7. Saint John
8. The 24 Old Men of the Apocalypse
9. Crist resuscitated
10. Saint Matthew
11. The Column
12. The Cross
13. The Crown of Thorns
14. Saint Luke
15. Saint Mark
16. The Nails and the Crown of Christ

7. The Condemnation and the Jug of Vinegar
8. Whip and scourges
9. The spear and the sponge
20. The angels lead the Just, in the form of children, towards Glory
21. Capital representing the Temptations of Christ
22. The prophets Jeremiah, Daniel, Isaiah and Moses
23. The Apostle James
24. The Apostles: Peter, Paul, James and John
25. Capital representing the Holy Trinity
26. Christ's family tree
27. *Santo dos Croques* (adjoining the rear of the mullion). The figure is traditionally held to be that of the *Maestro* Mateo
28. The Just are taken by the angels to the House of God
29. In the keys of the arch, Christ and the Archangel Gabriel
30. The Damned
31. Two Apostles
32. The Apostles Saint Bartholomew and Saint Thomas

Cathedral: nave.

arch is divided by the mullion, made up of two columns supported by a single base. In the middle of these is a statue of James, who seems to thank pilgrims for coming here to worship him. Lower down is Christ's family tree, in which David and Solomon can be recognised. By tradition, visitors carry out two rituals with regard to the mullion. The first is to place their hand on David's feet and make a wish. The second is for all those who wish to increase their intelligence, who should give their heads a bang («croque») three times against the statue of the «Santo dos Croques», traditionally said to be a representation of the *maestro* Mateo.

At first, the Portico of La Gloria gave onto the outside, following the custom of many churches built during the Middle Ages, though the original idea was somewhat spoiled in the 16th century, when the doors were installed.

The interior of the Cathedral has remained basically faithful to its original conception. The harmony of its arches, resting on majestic columns, and the atmosphere of tranquillity the temple breathes inspire visitors to take their time in admiring the building. One of its most outstanding features is the imposing **Capilla Mayor,** whose canopy, designed by Vega y Verdugo in baroque style, takes its inspiration from that in Saint Peter's in Rome, and forms a striking contrast to the simplicity of the Romanesque Cathedral. The niche contains

Capilla Mayor.

Silver urn containing the relics of the Apostle.

the famous silver plated statue of Saint James, and is reached from one side of the ambulatory to allow visitors to give the saint the traditional embrace.

Another passage leads down into the **Crypt of the Capilla Mayor,** containing in an ornate silver urn the relics of Saint James and his disciples, Theodore and Athanasius. The crypt, remodelled and opened for the Xacobeo of 1885, also conserves remains of the original 1st-century Roman building.

The ambulatory is surrounded by chapels of outstanding beauty and interest. Beginning on the right-hand side, we first come to the **Chapel of El Pilar,** originally designed as a sacristy, but finally converted into the mausoleum of Archbishop Monroy. The chapel features marble and jasper from Opporto, a baroque altarpiece by Casas y Novoa and countless coats of arms of Spain, of the basilica and of Monroy himself. Next is the **Chapel of Mondragón,** where we can admire a Flemish-style terra cotta pietà, whilst adjoining this is the **Chapel of La Azucena** or of Doña Mencia, containing the tomb of the latter. We then come to the door known as the Puerta Santa, or Puerta de los Perdones, flanked by two stone sculptures made in the workshops of the *maestro* Mateo. In the centre of the ambulatory is the **Chapel of El Salvador,** or of Saint Louis, King of France, which is where work on the basilica began and where confession was heard for foreign pilgrims. The Plateresque altarpiece contains a Romanesque sculpture of Our Lord revealing his Wounds. The **Chapel of Nuestra Señora la Blanca** features a Gothic altarpiece. This chapel has a Plateresque altarpiece containing a Romanesque sculpture of the Saviour showing his wounds. The final chapels in the ambulatory are that dedicated to Saint John the Apostle **(Capilla de San Juan Apóstol),** with its Romanesque entrance, and the **Chapel of San Bartolomé,** a veritable meeting-point between the Romanesque style of its groundplan and the Plateresque of its altar.

Chapel of El Pilar.

Chapel of El Espíritu Santo.

Continuing towards the Azabachería, we come to the **Chapel of La Concepción,** with Plateresque front; the **Chapel of El Espíritu Santo,** converted into that of La Virgen de la Soledad; and the **Chapel of San Andrés,** with baroque altar. Between these last two is the Chapel of Corticela, originally a church in its own right. The simplicity and intimacy of this space is in striking contrast with the sumptuousness of the rest of the basilica. It has a fine entrance doorway, Romanesque, its tympanum featuring an Adoration of the Magi. Worshippers in this chapel pray to the Virgin of Miracles or invoke the favour of Jesus of the Olive Grove, writing their prayers on paper, which they press into the hands of Jesus. Adjoining the Gate of Las Azabachería is the **Chapel of San Antonio,** with a fine 18th-century altarpiece, and the **Chapel of Lourdes** or of Santa Catalina, until the 16th century a royal pantheon.

In the left-hand aisle is the **Chapel of La Comunión,** a neoclassical work with a circular shape featuring motifs relating to the University, due to the fact that, from 1561 to 1734, this was where the academic titles granted by the university were awarded., and the **Chapel of El Cristo de Burgos,** whose groundplan is in the form of a Greek cross. Its dome features various coats of arms, whilst in the centre is a copy of the famous Christ of Burgos.

Romanesque door leading to the Chapel of La Corticela.

Cathedral cloister.

In the right-hand aisle, known as that of the Epistle, is a passage or vestibule containing the burial stone of Teodomiro, bishop of Iria Flavia and «discoverer» of the tomb of the Apostle in the early-9th century. This vestibule leads to the **Chapel of the Relics,** where the royal pantheon was transferred. It has a Gothic vault and the relics it contains include various small statues of Saint James, the «Caput Argentum», or bust-reliquary with the head of Santiago Alfeo (14th century), a Renaissance bust of Saint Pauline and a Christ bound to a column by Gaspar Becerra, dating to the late-16th century.

Opposite is the entrance to the **Chapel of San Fernando,** which now houses the Cathedral **Treasure** and forms part of the Cathedral Museums. The collection includes such pieces as the monstrance of Antonio of Arfe, a Renaissance work made from 60 kilos of gilt silver, and the monstrance-ostentorium donated by Archbishop Monroy, a work which harmoniously combines emeralds and sapphires.

The Cathedral cloister and the other dependencies of the

Cathedral Museums are reached from Plaza del Obradoiro. The ground floor and mezzanine are given over to an archaeological museum centred particularly on works pertaining to the Cathedral. The **cloister** itself is considered a masterpiece of Spanish Plateresque art. Each of its sides, containing columns and flying buttresses, is 40 metres in length, whilst under its floors rest the mortal remains of numerous Galician nobles. Passing through the cloister, we come to the **Chapterhouse,** with a flat, painted vault and a Rococo carving of Saint James, and the **Library,** which houses the botafumeiro, one of the most emblematic and best-loved objects in the Cathedral,

The botafumeiro, *censer, is kept in the Cathedral Library.*

Medical Faculty, in Rúa de San Francisco.

and a replica of the same. This censer, by José Losada, and dating back to 1851, is the largest in the world, weighing 80 kilos and with a height of 1.60 metres. It began to be used in the 14th century to perfume the air, lessening the odour of sweat from the pilgrims after their long journeys. In gilt brass, it is a veritable spectacle to see this great censer swinging down the nave and aisles of the crossing, guided by various men, known as traboleiros.

This visit ends at the **Tapestry Museum,** which has cartoons by Goya and Rubens, amongst other artists, and at the **balconada,** or covered gallery, commanding excellent views over Plaza del Obradoiro. The rest of the Cathedral, that is to say, the different outer doorways, is described in the next route in our guide.

In the square once more, we suggest ending this route with a visit to the Convent of San Francisco. Skirting around the Hostal de los Reyes Católicos, we take Rúa de San Francisco, in which stands the magnificent building which houses the **Faculty of Medicine (7),** built between 1910 and 1920. This road, with split levels, culminates at the monument to Saint

Francis, by Asorey, adjoining which is the **Convent of San Francisco de Valdediós (8)** which, though reformed in the 18th century dates back to the 17th, and was designed by Simón Rodriguez.

The neoclassical façade is divided into two sections, in the lower of which the entrance is framed by four columns resting on great basements, presided over by a statue of Saint Francis by José Ferreiro. The upper section features a large window over which is a pediment crowned by a cross guarded by angels. The interior of the church, with its classical air, is considered to be one of the finest baroque churches in Compostela.

Convent of San Francisco de Valdediós.

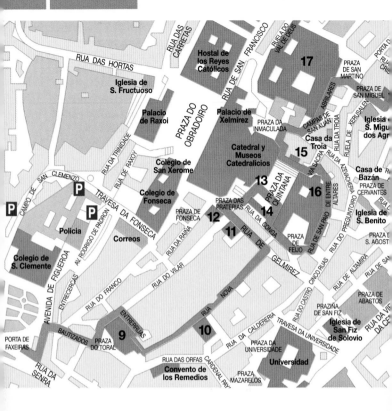

II FROM PORTA FAXEIRA TO SAN MARTÍN PINARIO

9. Palace of Bendaña
10. Church of Santa María de Salomé
11. Dean's House
12. Chapterhouse
13. Puerta Santa
14. Canons' House
15. Casa de la Parra
16. Convent of San Paio de Anteaitares
17. Monastery of San Martín Pinario
18. Pilgrimage Museum

As its name indicates, **Porta Faxeira** was where one of the seven gates of the old walled city formerly stood. It has now become one of the most popular meeting-places in

Compostela, and a busy thoroughfare towards La Ferradura or the city centre. Practically the entire historic centre is pedestrian, and its medieval air is also well-preserved. Initiatives are constantly made to ensure that houses needing restoration or rehabilitation do not lose their original physiognomy.

Porta Faxeira forms the origin of one of the most typical and emblematic streets in the old part of Santiago: **Rúa do Franco,** which continues to Plaza del Obradoiro. This street contains many bars and restaurants where the most demanding gourmets will be fully satisfied. Its name derives from the many French immigrants who established themselves here attracted by the economic boom which occurred during the construction of the new city.

Further on, Rúa do Franco gives way to **Rúa da Raiña** («of the queen»), called thus, in honour of Isabel of Portugal, who came to the city as a pilgrim. Other sources, however, attribute the street's name to Doña Urraca, whose turbulent life was much linked to Compostela.

A view of Rúa do Franco.

Palace of Bendaña, in Plaza del Toral.

From Porta Faxeira, taking Calle Bautizados, we come to **Plaza del Toral,** an irregularly-shaped yet harmonious square with central fountain. Concerts often take place at night in this space. On one side of the square is the **Palace of Bendaña (9),** built in the 18th century by Fernández Sarela. This elegant baroque building is crowned by a sculpture of Atlas holding up the world which, according to wicked tongues, he will drop when a virtuous woman passes under him.

We now take **Rúa do Vilar.** Like neighbouring Rúa Nova, this street is characterised by its elegant arcades, each of them different from the others, and which form a singular spectacle at dusk, as they begin to be lit up by romantic lamps. They also provide excellent shelter from the Compostela rain. There was a time when some of these arcades were pulled down in obedience of council regulations, but many were saved thanks to the stubborn refusal of the householders to comply.

Rúa do Vilar, which stretches to Plaza de las Platerías, was the street chosen by many of the city's leading citizens to install themselves. Here were concentrated jewellers', bookshops, silversmiths, hat-shops, and so on, giving the street a commercial air which it still retains. Narrow **Callejón de Entrerrúas** leads into **Rúa Nova,** built by Xelmírez in the 12th century to house immigrants arriving in the city. At number 44 we come to the **Palace of Ramirans,** the former College of Saint Patrick of the Irish, founded by Philip II as a centre for Irish students, countering the advance of Anglican reforms. Inside is a statue of Saint Patrick, patron saint of Ireland, reminding visitors of the original function of the building. Opposite is the **Church of**

Rúa do Vilar.

Church of Santa María de Salomé.

Santa María de Salomé (10), the only church in Spain dedicated to the Apostle's mother. Founded in the 12th" century, over its Romanesque door is a 14th-century Gothic porch. The baroque tower crowning the building dates to the 18th century and is by José Crespo.

A little further up the street, at number 21, is the **Teatro Principal,** built in 1841 and now an important cultural centre. At number 12 is the **Casa de las Pomas** («Apple House»), its façade full of ornamental fruit and the relief of a vieira, scallop, the universal symbol of Jacobean pilgrimage. At number 9, we find the **Palacio de Santa Cruz,** a neoclassical building now occupied by the nuns of the Immaculate Mary.

In Rúa de Gelmírez is the so-called **Casa de la Balconada,** built in the second half of the 17th century and recently rehabilitated to house various university services. This street leads into Plaza de las Platerías and, on a corner with Rúa do Vilar, stands the **Casa del Deán (11).** This Dean's House is by Fernández Sarela in 1752 and is in Compostela baroque style. It now houses the Pilgrim's Office.

Plaza de las Platerías is baroque in overall style. Its name is due to the fact that the silversmiths' guild had its offices in this square, with workshops occupying the surrounding shops and streets. In the centre is the **Fuente de los Caballos,** a statue dating back to 1829 and in Italianate style. It is com-

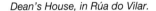

Dean's House, in Rúa do Vilar.

Porch of Las Platerías, in the square of the same name.

posed of four horses supporting an allegory of «Religion with the star over the arc of the Apostle». It is customary to throw a coin into the fountain and make a wish, though the water of the fount is also the scene of student fun and games.

The north side of the square is occupied by the Cathedral **Façade of the Platerías,** the only front conserving the original Romanesque work. Various master masons worked on this element, and the result is a fine sculptural composition in which stand out the reliefs of David playing the harp, the Saviour and Saint James among the cypresses. The typanum on the left features the Temptations of Christ, and that on the right, the Epiphany with the Magi. The construction to the left of the Pórtico de las Platerías corresponds to the outer walls of the cloister. This building, known as the Treasury Building, as it was here that the cathedral's most valuable pieces were kept, is crowned by the **Torre del Tesoro,** with a peculiar scaled apex which seems to imitate the form of the Aztec pyramids.

At the south side of this square is the **Casa del Cabildo (12),** or Chapterhouse, an admirable creation by Fernández Sarela. This has a false baroque front which is three metres thick with Rococo elements built to complete and adorn the surrounding square. The last of the buildings in the square is that of the Bank of Spain, built in 1940.

The nearby **Plaza de la Quintana** is divided by a wide staircase into two zones: La Quintana de los Muertos («of the dead») and La Quintana de los Vivos («of the living»). Under the stone slabs of the former is an old cemetery once famed as being buried here meant spending eternity beside the tomb of the Apostle.

This wide and lovely square is dominated by the **Clocktower** or Torre Berenguela, 72 metres in height. It was built in the late-

Plaza de Las Platerías.

Plaza de la Quintana with, in the background, the Casa de la Parra.

17th century by Domingo de Andrade. It is a moving experience to hear the slow, hoarse chimes of its clock in the midst of so much profusely-worked stone. Adjoining the tower, following the walls of the Cathedral rear, is the **Puerta Real,** framed by Doric columns and also by Domingo de Andrade, and the **Puerta Santa (13),** or Holy Door. This door, also known as the Puerta del Perdón, is flanked by 24 statues representing Biblical characters from the choirstalls, now lost, carved in stone by the maestro Mateo, and, above, the Apostle, dressed in the robes of a pilgrim and flanked by his disciples Theodore and Athanasius. The door is only opened in jubilee years, when the archbishop knocks on it with a silver hammer.

The south side of the square contains the **Casa de la Conga (14),** or Canons' House, built in the 17th century by Domingo de Andrade and Casas Novoa. Its Italianate porticoes support graceful semicircular arches and peculiar chimneys, those constant elements in the Compostela urban landscape.

The upper part of the square, «La Quintana de los Vivos»,

contains the **Casa de la Parra (15),** its front adorned with carved stone fruit motifs mixed with the real vines and grapes which give the house its name. The building has an interesting cube-shaped chimney.

Opposite the side of the Cathedral, closing the square to the east, the rounded wall extends, with the many grilled windows of the cells forming part of the **Convent of San Paio de Antealtares (16).** In the middle of the sombre wall, a plaque renders homage to the «Literary Battalion», students from Santiago who fought against Napoleon. The origins of the convent go back to the years immediately after the discovery

Puerta Santa.

of the tomb of Saint James, when King Alphonse II ordered the Benedictines to tend and watch over the holy site, whose nearness to the Cathedral gives it the name of Antealtares. The present building, dating to the 17th century, replaced the original church constructed at the king's command. The convent was occupied by Benedictine monks until the 16th century, when it was taken over by nuns from the same order. Its present inhabitants are famed even today for the exquisite, home-made sweets and pastries they produce.

Circling this great building in the surrounding streets, we can admire its different fronts: that of Plaza Feixóo is by Lucas Ferro Caaveiro and features a sculpture of the Flight to Egypt; that of Calle de San Paio, by Melchor Velasco, gives access to the revolving doors. The entrance to the convent church is from the Vía Sacra, near Plaza de la Quintana. The church has a fine altarpiece and a magnificent organ, played by the nuns in the evening. From the church we can enter the **Museum of**

Monastery of San Paio de Antealtares, Plaza de Feixóo entrance.

Front of the Monastery of San Martín Pinario.

Sacred Art, a small museum with interesting pieces such as holy vestments, carvings and other religious objects.

Back in the square again, we take Travesía de la Quintana to reach **Plaza de la Inmaculada.** On the left is the north front of the Cathedral, or **Puerta de la Azabachería,** with its Rococo elements, whilst opposite stands the **Monastery of San Martín Pinario (17).** This huge monastery, which occupies an area of around 20,000 square metres, dates back to the 16th century. It was formerly a Benedictine monastery, inhabited by monks from nearby San Paio de Antealtares, and since the last century has been the seat of the *Seminario Mayor,* though in summer it serves as a hotel.

The main front, some 100 metres in length, is by Fray Gabriel de las Casas and Casas Novoa and follows the classical taste of the time. The front is framed by two pairs of Doric columns and crowned by a frontispiece which features the coat of arms of Spain and, above this, an equestrian statue of Saint Martin,

Church of San Martín Pinario.

flanked by angels, tearing up his cloak to help a beggar. The interior features a fine processional cloister and the old granaries. It is said that these were never empty of grain and that the wise management of this wealth allowed the Benedictines to undertake extending this monumental monastery in the 18th century.

The monastery church is entered from nearby Plaza de San Martín. Designed by Mateo López, though later modified, it is one of the finest examples of baroque art in the city. The entrance to the church is by an unusual descending flight of steps. The church has a groundplan in the form of a Latin cross, and makes excellent use of the light which enters through its ribbed dome. The outstanding feature in the interior is the richly-ornamented high altarpiece, by various artists under the direction of Casas Novoa. Also interesting are the organs, the choirstalls, the sacristy and various of the chapels, which combine to make this church an exceptional museum of baroque art.

In nearby Plaza de San Miguel, opposite the neoclassical Church of San Miguel dos Agros, is the **Pilgrimage Museum (18),** installed in the 14th-century Gothic Palace of Don Pedro.

High altarpiece of San Martín Pinario.

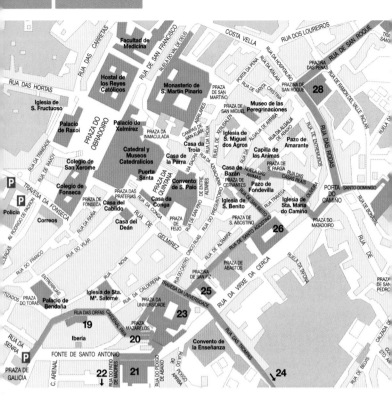

III. FROM PLAZA DE GALICIA TO THE CONVENT OF SANTA CLARA

19. Convent of Las Huérfanas or of Los Remedios
20. Arch of Mazarelos
21. Convent of Las Mercedarias Descalzas
22. Santa María la Real del Sar
23. The University
24. Convent of Belvís
25. San Fiz de Solovio
26. Church of San Agustín
27. Santo Domingo de Bonaval and the Museum of the Galician People
28. Hospital of San Roque
29. Convent of Santa Clara

Plaza de Galicia stands at the limits of where once stretched the city walls. To the south lies the new city, facing us is the historic centre. This square features the building now occupied by the Hotel Compostela, in olden days the seat of the Inquisition. Opposite is **Porta Mámoa,** whose Galician name refers to the typical funeral monuments used here during the Bronze Age. Rúa das Orfas begins here with, on the corner with Rúa de Fonte de Santo Antonio, the Café Derby, notable as it preserves intact the atmosphere of the turn of the century. This is one of the few remaining «debating cafés», formerly abundant in the city.

Rúa das Orfas takes its name from the former **Convent of Las Huérfanas or of Los Remedios (19),** which stands at number 5. It was built at the beginning of the 18th century by order of Archbishop Sanclemente to take in orphan girls. This simple building features a fine cloister and a belltower, by Casas y

Convent of Las Huérfanas or of Nuestra Señora de los Remedios.

Convent of Las Madres Mercedarias.

Novoa, who also designed the front. The church contains a remarkable baroque altarpiece by Francisco de Lens, with carvings by Gambino, and the carved white marble tomb of Cardinal Martín de Herrera, by Asorey.

Calle Cardenal Payá leads us to Plaza de Mazarelos. To the right is the **Arch of Mazarelos (20),** the only city gate which conserves the original wall and through which wine was brought into Compostela. Opposite, once more outside the old city walls, is the **Convent of Las Madres Mercedarians (21),** founded in the 17th century by Archbishop Andrés Girón. The front of the building is divided into two sections flanked by two columns. The upper section is based on a semicircular arch, over which is a large window. The lower section contains a doorway with three entrances leading into the simple interior of the church, which has a single nave, its groundplan in the shape of a Latin cross. Over the centre of the crossing is a large, graceful dome.

From here, taking Rúa do Patio de Madres, an optional route would lead us –though at a distance of two or three kilometres– to the **Collegiate Church of Santa María la Real del Sar (22).** This Romanesque monument was built in the 12th century by Canon Munio Alfonso and consecrated by Archbishop Xelmírez. Its situation by the River Sar, surrounded by vegetation, give the site a particular charm.

The church is not only one of the city's most beautiful churches, but also one of the most surprising due to the disconcerting inclination of the columns supporting the vaults. It seems that the instability of the land and the excessive height of the aisles caused the inclination of the supporting pillars, giving the interior of the building a dreamlike quality. Robust flying buttresses were added in the 16th century to shore up the building. Also interesting is the cloister, which conserves one side, made up of nine arches, from the original Romanesque construction, attributed to the workshop of the maestro Mateo. A small Parish Museum has been installed here, exhibiting collections of silverwork, Romanesque sculptures and priceless parchment documents.

Collegiate Church of Santa María la Real del Sar.

Faculty of Journalism in Plaza de Mazarelos.

We now retrace our steps to Plaza de Mazarelos. The square is presided over by a statue of Eugenio Montero Ríos (1832-1914), Galician jurist and liberal politician. Next we come to the Journalism Faculty of the **University of Compostela (23).** The present building, dating back to the 18th century and designed by Simón Rodríguez, was built as an annex to the former College of the Company of Jesus for primary education and the study of letters and grammar. Over the door is the coat of arms of the founder of the college, Archbishop Yermo.

In adjoining Plaza de la Universidad is the **Church of La Compañía,** later converted into the Church of La Universidad. On the front, in consequence of the persecution the Order was once subjected to, the statues of Saint Ignatius and Saint Francis Xavier have been replaced by those of Saint Peter and Saint Paul. Inside is a spectacular altarpiece by Simón Rodríguez in 1720, its exuberant forms soaring up to the very ceiling. At the top is God, in His hands the destiny of the world. Below is the Eucharist in the form of a sky blue vault, and the statue of the Virgin as if floating in the clouds.

We next come to the University of Santiago **Faculty of Geography and History**, a building designed by Miguel Ferro Caaveiro and built in the late-18th century, though altered in the 19th and 20th centuries, on the site of the novitiate of the Company of Jesus. The original purpose of the building was as the university central offices. The front of the building, in a more classicist style, is by Melchor de Prado. In it is represented an allegory of Wisdom, whilst the cornice has sculptures representing important benefactors of the institution. The interior, organised around a wide cloister, contains an excellent library (second floor) and a fine central hall, decorated with frescoes by Fenollera and González.

Opposite the university building, on the corner with Rúa do Calderería, is one of Compostela's most typical restaurants, O Asesino. This traditional restaurant, with wood-fired oven, was a favourite with the writer Valle Inclán, and offers tasty home-made dishes.

We now continue along Travesía da Universidade, where a statue of Alphonse II reminds us that this was the first king to make a pilgrimage to Santiago, taking Rúa das Trompas until

Central hall of the University of Compostela.

Convent of Belvís.

we come to the **Convent of Belvís (24),** which stands on a small hill surrounded by green fields. Founded in 1305 by Doña Teresa González for descalced Dominican nuns, this simple grey granite monument was rebuilt in the late-17th century by Fray Gabriel de las Casas, whilst the church was designed by Casas y Novoa. From the original is conserved the Chapel of La Virgen del Portal, dedicated to a Virgin to whom the faithful of Compostela are greatly devoted. As with other churches in the city, evensong is a particularly beautiful event.

Returning to Travesía da Universidade, we stop to admire the **Church of San Fiz de Solovio (25),** a tiny church, the oldest in the city. It was built in honour of Saint Paio, discoverer of the tomb of Saint James and was reconstructed centuries later by Simón Rodríguez, who also designed the belltower. Of the original church, there remain the portal, whose tympanum features a representation of the Epiphany, retaining some of its polychromy, and a number of slender columns crowned by splendid capitals. The baroque interior has the fine Altar of La Soledad and the tomb of Cardinal López González.

The tranquillity of the Church of San Fiz de Solovio is in stark contrast with the busy morning sessions of the **Plaza de Abastos,** or market. This site is made up of various stone-built pavilions dating to the 1940s, imitation Romanesque in style, and which harmonise perfectly with the architectural setting. The main attraction of the market is the busy activity which goes on there, and the wares of the many stalls.

At the other end of the market can be made out the imposing silhouette of the **Church of San Agustín (26),** adjoining the former Augustinian Convent, built in the 17th century and acquired in the early-20th century by the Jesuits, who used it

Church of San Fiz de Solovio.

Church of San Agustín.

as a university residence and college. The enormous cloister, supported by Doric columns, is by Jácome Fernández. The Churrigueresque front of the church is flanked by two towers, one of which is unfinished. The front features a statue of the Virgen de la Cerca, patron saint of a chapel which formerly stood on this site.

The nearby **Plaza de Cervantes** was formerly the principal centre of city life, known in those days as Praza do Pan or Praza do Campo. It has had its present name since a monument dedicated to that writer was placed here. The square is surrounded by noble buildings, such as the Palace of Fondevila and the Casa de Bazán, and a church dedicated to Saint Bieito, a neoclassical work originally founded in the 10th century. Of the reforms carried out by Xelmírez in the 12th century there remains the polychrome Gothic tympanum with a representation of the Epiphany. Close by is the 17th-century **Chapel of Las Animas,** which features an unusual pediment depicting the tormenting of the souls by eternal fire.

Rúa das Casas Reais leads us to **Porta do Camiño,** formerly the site of one of the seven gates in the old city walls, entry point of pilgrims taking the French Way. Opposite, we climb up to the **Convent of Santo Domingo de Bonaval (27),** whose dependencies now house the **Museum of the Galician People.** It was built in the 13th century after the saint's second pilgrimage to Santiago. Archbishop Monroy later converted the monastery into a hospice and school for the deaf and dumb.

Convent of Santo Domingo de Bonaval, seat of the Museum of the Galician People.

The interior of the church, which contains 13th-16th century elements, is an excellent example of the transition from Romanesque to Gothic. On the left-hand side is the Pantheon of Illustrious Galicians, containing the tombs of such important personages in the history of Galicia as Francisco Asorey, Alfonso Rodríguez Castelao and the outstanding figure in Galician letters, Rosalía de Castro. The façade is by Domingo de Andrade, who also designed the most outstanding part of the convent: the Façade of the Portería, the cloister, the rooms and the famous spiral staircase, built by Andrade in three concentric sections to form a spectacular exercise in geometrical composition. This staircase provides entrance to the museum and terminates in a viewpoint looking out over the city.

The Museum of the Galician People was installed here in 1976. Both entertaining and easy to understand, the museum offers an ethnological and anthropological guide to the different regions of Galicia. Its rooms are dedicated to such subjects as the sea, the fields, country and city trades, habitat and architecture, popular ceramics, literature, music and dance and popular costumes. There are also rooms for temporary

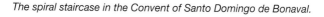

The spiral staircase in the Convent of Santo Domingo de Bonaval.

The Museum of the Galician People presents the most varied aspects of Galician culture.

Hospital of San Roque.

exhibitions, a concert hall and video library, documentation and bibliography departments, and a restoration and conservation section. The convent is surrounded by pleasant gardens and opposite is the modern building housing the **Galician Centre for Contemporary Art.**

Once more in Porta do Camiño, Rúa das Rodas leads us to the Praziña de San Roque. The **Hospital de San Roque (28)** was ordered built by Archbishop Francisco Blanco in the 16th century to provide relief during an epidemic of plague. The portal of this modest, white-walled building, designed by

Gaspar de Arce, features the coat of arms of the founder and two sculptures representing Saint Damian and Saint Cosme, two committed health workers who made up for the short-comings of their medical skills through prayer. The interior of the building has a cloister of Doric columns and a chapel, dedicated to the saint, with an ornate altarpiece by Simón Rodríguez.

Rúa San Roque runs into that of Santa Clara, thus named in honour of the **Convent of Santa Clara (29),** founded by Queen Violante, wife of Alphonse X, the Wise, in the 13th century, though the present building dates to the late-18th. The most notable feature is a false façade, seven metres deep, by Simón Rodríguez, following the canons of so-called «plate baroque». The result, for many a veritable precursor of Cubism, gives the sensation that the frontispiece could fall at any moment. A corridor and courtyard lead to the church itself, which has an altarpiece by Domingo de Andrade.

Convent of Santa Clara.

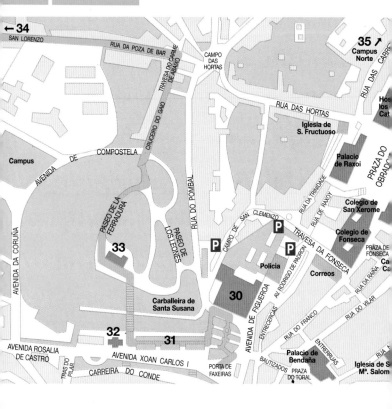

IV. LA ALAMEDA AND ENVIRONS

30. College of San Clemente
31. Paseo de la Alameda
32. Church of El Pilar
33. Hermitage of Santa Susana
34. San Lorenzo de Trasouto
35. Auditorium of Galicia

If until now our routes have proposed itineraries exclusively inside the historic centre of Compostela, this next route will allow us to discover, on the one hand, the part of the city which has grown up outside the walls and, on the other, the exuberant park formed by the Ferradura Gardens, a paradise of green contrasting with the profusion of carved stone of the old city.

Our starting-point is Porta Faxeira. Starting out towards Paseo de la Alameda, in Rúa do Pombal we see on our right the main front of the **College of San Clemente (30),** founded by the Cordoban Archbishop Sanclemente in 1602 to provide accommodation for Galician and Cordoban students. This simple building with its wide courtyard is the work of architects Jácome Fernández and Leonel de Avalle. Over the years, it has served as the seat of various university faculties, as well as museum and library. It currently houses the Rosalía de Castro School.

The structure of **Paseo de la Alameda (31)** reproduces the hierarchy which formerly existed in society. The centre was reserved for the nobility, the working classes took the right-hand side, and the clergy, old people and professors walked on the left. Halfway along is the Modernist bandstand, designed by García Vaamonde and considered one of the finest in Spain. A little further along is the **Church of Nuestra Señora del Pilar (32),** a simple baroque church dating back to the 18th century and which completes Paseo de la Alameda on this side, whilst to the south the new districts of the city stretch out

College of San Clemente.

Monument to Rosalía de Castro, and a view of the Ferradura Gardens.

Panoramic view of the city and Cathedral from Paseo de la Ferradura.

before us. The front, flanked by two towers, is presided over by a statue of the Virgin.

From here, a stairway adjoining a fountain lead us up to the **Ferradura Gardens.** This park, with its copses of hundred-year-old oaks, was given to the city by the Count of Altamira. A stroll in the shade of its tall trees, stopping to rest on one of the many benches, is a deeply-rooted custom in Compostela. The park also contains monuments to Méndez Núñez, Archbishop Figueroa, Rosalía de Castro and Pais Lapido. The presence of these last two writers gives this last stretch of the walk its name Paseo de las letras Gallegas, or Path of Galician Letters. The eastern section of the gardens commands splendid views over the city and the Cathedral. The visit culminates in the so-called Paseo de los Leones, which takes its name from the lions carved by Francisco Linares and which have guarded the park entrance since 1885.

The Ferradura Gardens Surround an old pre-Roman mound crowned by the **Hermitage of Santa Susana (33),** dedicated to the co-patron saint of Santiago and consecrated by Xelmírez

Hermitage of Santa Susana.

in 1102. Of the original structure, built in the 12th century, there remains only the simple Romanesque portico. The present building dates back to the 17th century, whilst the belltower was installed in 1885. Its presence at the top of the mound gives it something of a rural air and a special charm, despite its proximity to the city. Over the years, the relics and the remains of Saint Susan were removed from the interior to be taken to the Cathedral, and its functions as a parish church were also transferred to the Church of Nuestra Señora del Pilar.

From the east side of the Ferradura Gardens we can make out the **University Campus.** Designed by Jenaro de la Fuente, the campus was built in 1930 and, conceived as a huge, extensive open space, forms a powerful contrast with the narrow labyrinth of the old city centre.

After Rúa da Poza de Bar we come to the Carballeira de San Lourenzo and, hidden by a leafy oak wood, the **Monastery of San Lorenzo de Trasouto (34).** This was founded in the 13th century by Bishop Martín Arias of Zamora. After many years as a Franciscan monastery, the Mendizábal disentailment led to its becoming the property of the Duchess of Medina de las Torres, who had it converted into a palace. The fine side entrance, with a statue of Saint Lawrence, dates to this period. The original Romanesque portico is conserved, as are the tombs of the marquises of Ayamonte, made from white Carrara marble.

The Campus Norte contains one of the most innovative exponents of recent Compostela architecture, the **Auditorium of Galicia (35).** This building, composed of great cubic blocks and surrounded by an artificial lake, is a clear indication that the city is not content to rest on its historic laurels.

Continuing in a northerly direction, we find, in the wood known as the «Selva Negra» («Black Forest»), the tiny Hermitage of San Paio del Monte. From here and on the banks of the River Sarela, emerges **Monte Pedroso,** on which we can make out the *Via Crucis,* which was ordered placed here by Cardinal Martín de Herrera, and enjoy splendid views over the city.

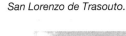

San Lorenzo de Trasouto.

Seafood is one of the pillars of Galician cuisine.

GASTRONOMY

The *cuisine* of Galicia and, by extension, of Santiago, is rightly famed for the exquisiteness of its dishes. The local fish and seafood is well-known, but the meat and vegetables obtained from these lands are also excellent, as are the tasty cheeses from the Ulla Valley and the choice pork from Sarria, the bases of dishes whose deliciousness is even further heightened if accompanied by the pleasant wines of Albariño or Ribeiro.

These tasty foods, often cooked in the simplest of ways following traditional old recipes, are available at most of the city's restaurants. Fish is traditionally prepared in the form of «caldeirada», cooked with vegetables, potatoes and peppers and seasoned with paprika, oil and garlic. Lobster, prawns, barnacles and crab all share the bill with fruits of the sea more specific to Compostela, such as «vieira» (scallops) and «santiaguiños», marked with the cross of Saint James. Not forgetting, of course, the celebrated «pulpo gallego», octopus simply cooked and exquisite to the palate. As regards meat dishes, one of the most delicious is «lacón con grelos», a tasty, healthy stew made from the tender leaves of turnip tops and pork and which was but recently incorporated into Galician *cuisine*. Other local delicacies include the famous «empanada», pastry made from wheat flour and filled with eggs, vegetables, meat, sausage or fish; and cheese, generally in the form of *tetilla* («teat»).

As regards wine, Albariño and Ribeiro wines are light, fresh and a little acidic, whilst Galicia's most typical liqueur is «orujo».

Turning to desserts, Compostela's most authentic gastronomic product is the so-called «Tarta Real» or «Tarta de Santiago», made from almond flour and sprinkled with castor sugar, in which is drawn the cross of Saint James.

Tarta de Santiago.

The botafumeiro takes on especial splendour during the Feast of Saint James.

FESTIVITIES

Compostela lives its fiestas and celebration with great passion and fervour. Carnival, Holy Week, Ascension –between May and June– or the Feast of the Assumption –15 August– all these are major dates in the calendar in Santiago. However, the city's festivity *par excellence* is that held in honour of the Apostle James, which last throughout the second fortnight of July. A full programme of religious and leisure activities spark off a veritable explosion of joy when the streets of the city are invaded by celebrating merry-makers. The festivities strike an even higher not, however, in Jacobean years, that is, when 25 July falls on a Sunday. The culminating moments are the firework display which takes place on 24 July, the traditional offering to the Apostle and the prodigious swinging of the *botafumeiro* in the Cathedral.

ARTS AND CRAFTS

Until just a few years ago, crafts were one of the main pillars of the economy of Compostela and, even today, many traditional workshops continue to ply their trade. Of these, the manufacture of jet trinkets is the most traditional and original to Santiago. Jet –hard, black coal, a variant of lignite– is made into *figas* (amulets against the evil eye), necklaces, rosaries, crosses or tiny images of Saint James. Nonetheless, pottery is the craft industry which has developed most in recent years. The city's many ceramicists have adapted their work to suit current tastes and needs. For their part, the local silversmiths continue to produce silver and jet articles of the highest quality, specialising particularly in miniature *botafumeiros,* medals and other mementoes of Saint James.

Miniature statues of the Apostle, a typical souvenir of Compostela.

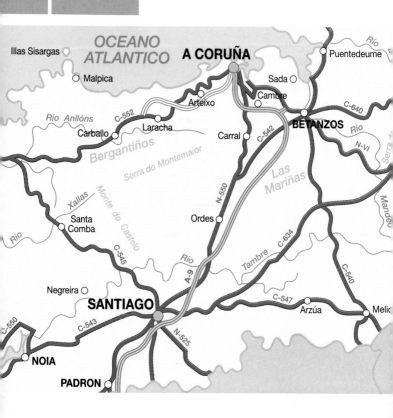

EXCURSIONS

If Santiago envelops us in the magic of its monumental forms, Galicia, its landscapes tinted with intense blues and greens, seduces us with the magic of its fields, *rías,* towns and villages. We shall here just recommend a few excursions from the city of Compostela.

Around 20 kilometres from Santiago is **Padrón,** a borough with a population of around 4,000 whose history is closely-linked to Jacobean traditions and to the world of letters. According to tradition, in the 1st century AD, Saint James preached in these fertile lands between the Sar and Ulla rivers. Padrón is also the birth-place of many writers of enormous prestige, among them Nobel prize-winner Camilo José Cela, from nearby Iria-Flavia, and Galicia's most outstanding poet, Rosalía de Castro. The house where the latter lived and died (on 15 July 1885), now converted into a museum, is open to the public. The writer's house, known as La Matanza, is a typical large Galician rural dwelling. The House-Museum contains objects, mementoes and private effects of the author of «Follas Novas» («New Leaves»). Outstanding of the rest of Padrón is the noble baroque town hall, built in the 18th century, with a beautiful staircase, and the Palace of the Bishop of Quito, both found in the historic centre of the town. Padrón is also famous for its Herbón green peppers, reputedly brought here from Mexico in the 16th century by Franciscan monks. Planted in the valley, they become more and more spicy as the summer goes on.

Not far from Padrón, though bathed by the Atlantic, is **Noia,** a small town of remote origins whose moment of greatest prosperity occurred during the 15th and 16th centuries, when it was active as a military and commercial port. Noia corresponds has the structure of a medieval city, formerly surrounded by walls with twelve gates. Some houses from that period are still conserved in Noia, and the old centre boasts its most emblematic buildings. Outstanding is the Church of Santa María a Nova, dated 1327, surrounded by a guild

«La Matanza», Rosalía de Castro House-Museum, in Padrón.

Noia. Church of Santa María.

cemetery in whose tombstones, some as early as the 10th century, are engraved the emblems of each guild. There are also two interesting cruceiros (calvaries), on Gothic and that of El Humilladeiro, standing on four columns and richly decorated. In the north of the province, perched on a hill, is the city of **Betanzos,** one of the most beautiful in Galicia. Medieval in layout, it conserves the remains of its old city walls. Its centre was declared of national historic and artistic interest in 1970. Adjoining the busy Plaza dos Irmáns García Naveira, also known as «O Campo» –the field– is the Convent of Santo Domingo with its baroque tower, now the Museum of As Mariñas. Opposite are the Archives of the Kingdom of Galicia, a neoclassical building dating back to the reign of Charles III. In Plaza de la Constitución is the Church of Santiago, a Gothic building with various Romanesque elements and a fine equestrian statue of Saint James at the entrance.

However, the most interesting monuments in Betanzos are the Churches of San Francisco and of Santa María do Azogue, two Gothic edifices standing together in a square with a cruceiro between them. The former contains many magnificent tombs of local nobles, including that of Fernán Pérez de Andrade. The Church of Santa María do Azogue has a splendid 18th-century baroque altarpiece.

With a population of around 250,000, **La Coruña** shares political, cultural and economic dominance in Galicia with Santiago de Compostela. This is one of the most ancient cities in the region, its history dotted with enthralling legends about the early Celtic settlements, ruled by the caudillo Breogán. In Roman times, the city was an important port on the route to the British Isles, an importance as a seafaring city which reached its height when the Invincible Armada sailed from its quays in 1588. A year later, La Coruña put up heroic resistance against the attacks of the English, led by Francis Drake. From these

Tomb of Fernán Pérez de Andrade, in the Church of San Francisco, Betanzos.

La Coruña: the port, and Avenida Marina.

events emerged the mythical figure of María Pita, who led the defenders of the city and whose bravery is commemorated each year during the August celebrations which take place in the city.

One or two centuries later, the British once more played a part in the history of the city, this time defending it against the attacks of the Napoleonic forces. The battle ended with the fall of La Coruña into French hands and the death of the English General John Moore, who is buried in the Garden of San Carlos. In the 19th century, the city flourished economically thanks to rapid industrialisation, and it is now a modern city with excellent infrastructure, its port the most important in Europe for fresh fish.

Its most characteristic streets are Avenida Marina, with its glazed galleries, and Rúa Real, the city's main commercial thoroughfare. Its monuments include the imposing Tower of

Hercules, the only Roman lighthouse surviving in the world. With a square groundplan, it stands at a height of 58 metres. The lighthouse was rebuilt in 1790.

The Paseo Marítimo, or sea front, embraces the isthmus on which the old part of the city stands. This monumental zone contains a harmonious assortment of architectural styles. Here, for instance, is the Church of Santiago, the oldest church in La Coruña, dating back to the 12-15th centuries, and the impressive City Hall, in Plaza Santa Pita. Rúas das Donas leads to the Collegiate Church of Santa María del Campo, built in the 12th and 13th centuries. From here, we can lose ourselves in the charming streets of Sinagoga, Cortaduría or Zapatería, reaching Plaza de las Bárbaras, one of the best-loved squares in the city in which stands the Convent of Las Madres Clarisas, the Church of Santo Domingo and the former Casa de la Moneda, or mint. Taking Rúa de San Francisco, we come to the Romantic Garden of San Carlos, commanding fine views over the city, of the *Ría* and of San Antón, an old 16th-century fortress which now houses the Historical and Archaeological Museum.

The Tower of Hercules.

CONTENTS

The visit to Santiago de Compostela 2
Historical introduction 4
General map of the city 8

ITINERARIES:

I The Plaza del Obradoiro and the Cathedral: 10
Hostal de los Reyes Católicos, Raxoi Palace,
Collège de San Xerome, College of Fonseca,
Xelmírez Palace, Cathedral and Cathedral Museums,
Faculty of Medicine, Convent of San Francisco de
Valdediós.

II From Porta Faxeira to San Martín Pinario: 36
Porta Faxeira, Rúa do Franco, Palace of Bendaña,
Rúa do Vilar, Rúa Nova, Church of Santa María de
Salomé, Dean's House, Plaza de las Platerías,
Chapterhouse, Plaza de la Quintana, Puerta Santa,
Canons' House, Casa de la Parra, Convent of San Paio
de Antealtares, Plaza de la Inmaculada, Monastery of
San Martín Pinario, Pilgrimage Museum.

III From Plaza de Galicia to Convent of Santa Clara: .50
Convent of Las Huérfanas or of Los Remedios, Arch of
Mazarelos, Convent of Las Madres Mercedarias,
Collegiate Church of Santa María la Real del Sar,
University, Convent of Belvís, Church of San Fiz de
Solovio, Plaza de Abastos, Church of San Agustín,
Plaza de Cervantes, Chapel of Las Animas, Convent of
Santo Domingo de Bonaval and Museum of the Galician
People, Hospital of San Roque, Convent of Santa Clara.

IV La Alameda and environs: 64
College of San Clemente, Paseo de la Alameda,
Church of Nuestra Señora del Pilar, Ferradura Gardens,
Hermitage of Santa Susana, University Campus,
Monastery of San Lorenzo de Trasouto, Auditorium of
Galicia.

Gastronomy 70

Festivities 72

Arts and crafts 73

Excursions:
Padrón 74
Noia 75
Betanzos 76
A Coruña 77

The printing of this book was completed
in the workshops of
FISA - ESCUDO DE ORO, S.A.
Palaudarias, 26 - Barcelona (Spain)